Susan Hampshire's
My Secret
Garden

THE NATIONAL GARDENS SCHEME

SUSAN HAMPSHIRE'S
MY SECRET GARDEN

SUSAN BERRY

PHOTOGRAPHY BY
HUGH PALMER

COLLINS & BROWN

IN ASSOCIATION WITH

GRANADA TELEVISION

First published in Great Britain in 1993 by
Collins & Brown Limited
Mercury House
195 Knightsbridge
London SW7 1RE

1 3 5 7 9 8 6 4 2

British Library Cataloguing-in-Publication Data:
A catalogue record for this book
is available from the British Library.
ISBN 1 85585 156 3

Conceived with the help of Charlotte Winby,
the producer and director of *My Secret Garden*, a series of programmes
screened as part of Granada Television's *This Morning* Programme,
which this book accompanies

Art Director: Roger Bristow
Designed by: Nigel Partridge
Illustrations by: Arthur Baker

Filmset by Spectrum, London
Reproduction by J. Film, Singapore
Printed and bound in Great Britain by the Bath Press

FRONTISPIECE *The garden at 25 Ellesmere Road.*

CONTENTS

- - ● - -

PREFACE

W HEN I WAS A CHILD, I was at my happiest sitting elbow-deep in grass cuttings in my father's wheelbarrow. My passion for gardening has grown ever since. I am not an expert, just an enthusiastic amateur, but this enthusiasm has afforded me hours of pleasurable hard work and relaxation. Gardening has recharged my batteries, enhanced my life, and made me feel happy to be alive.

There are many ways of learning about gardening, but one of the easiest is to visit other people's gardens, whether in person, through television, or through books such as this one. This is why the National Gardens Scheme, which will receive a royalty from the sales of this book, is such a wonderful idea and has proved to be so successful. There are now nearly 3,000 gardens belonging to the scheme and together they cover the whole spectrum of sizes and styles. While some are enormous, with parklands and six gardeners, others resemble pocket handkerchiefs and rely on a single pair of loving hands. By opening to the public on special days, they help raise money for a number of different charities — in particular the Queen's Nursing Institute.

The filming of *My Secret Garden* for Granada Television's *This Morning* programme was a job I can only describe as a delight. We travelled around the country, filming a new garden every day, and, at each one, the owners showed off their prized specimens, bemoaned the common enemies of cats, rabbits, slugs and moles, and shared the tricks of the trade and other secrets. I met wonderful people and picked up many handy tips which have since proved extremely useful in my own garden.

The television programmes also became the seeds of this book, which captures both the individuality and idiosyncracies of the gardens visited and highlights the mine of practical information offered by the owners.

SUSAN HAMPSHIRE

INTRODUCTION

⊥o those of you who are new to gardening, the use of Latin names for plants may seem like a deliberate attempt to mystify the inexperienced, but, in fact, botanists use Latin names to try to prevent confusion. It then becomes possible to identify any plant very precisely, according to its particular botanical features.

Plants with broadly similar characteristics are grouped into families, and within these families those that have specifically similar features — such as five-petalled flowers, for example — are subdivided into a further group. Each of these groups is called a *genus*, and this is the first name you see printed in Latin and in italics. So roses, for example, belong to the genus *Rosa*. Within each genus, the plants may differ from each other again in various ways, and these naturally occurring differences are grouped under *species* — which is the Latin name in italics that appears after the genus name — so you would find, for example, *Rosa filipes* and *Rosa macrophylla*. Within these species you may get variants again, and if they occur naturally, they will be given a further Latin name, whereas if a plant breeder has introduced these differences deliberately they will be given an English name, written in Roman and with quote marks around it — for example *Rosa filipes* 'Kiftsgate'. In some plants, where the variant is the result of crossing different species, you may simply get the genus name followed by the varietal name — *Rosa* 'Buff Beauty', for example.

Most good gardening books have an index at the back that gives you both the Latin name and the common, or English, name of the plant, so you should be able to find the equivalent name if you need to. Nurseries usually list plants under their Latin names, but occasionally they do not give the latest Latin names. Botanists are constantly finding new features in plants, which then get reclassified. If this happens, the plant is usually given both the old name and the new name for a while. The old name is put in brackets afterwards with the words 'syn.' in front, which stands for synonym.

Most libraries stock a wide range of gardening books, including some aimed specifically at novice gardeners. One of the best libraries of gardening books is held by the Royal Horticultural Society in London, to which members of the society have access. Anyone can join the RHS, for which they pay an annual subscription. The Royal Horticultural Society also publishes a range of books, including two 'bibles' — the *Encyclopaedia of Plants and Flowers* and the *Encyclopaedia of Gardening*.

No-one should be put off the idea of starting to garden. Most of it comes down to basic common sense, and observation. Anyone who has brought up children successfully will find that gardening requires many of the same skills — you need to give your charges regular food, water and attention, particularly to the messages they are giving you. If a plant looks unhappy and fails to thrive in a particular place, then move it, ideally when it is resting — in other words, not in spring or early summer during its most active growth period. Most of our best-known gardeners learned their skills on the job, from trial and error. They all admit to failures, but have carried on undeterred, and made a note not to make the same mistake again.

I hope the gardens in this book will whet your appetite, and either get you started as a gardener or encourage you to improve the garden you already have.

FORMAL GARDEN
HASELEY COURT

· · ● · ·

LEFT Clipped box spirals form a focal point in the ornamental walled garden, in which 'Ballerina' roses trained as standards make a vertical contrast above the perennial borders. Seen here is Lychnis coronaria, in its magenta and white forms, creeping jenny, phloxes and day lilies in one border, and bergenias in another.

THESE EXQUISITE TEN-ACRE GARDENS, surrounding a beautiful Queen Anne house, have something to offer everyone. They comprise a topiary garden (the jewel in its crown), a walled garden, a formal canal, a wild woodland area and a potager. It is all meticulously maintained and, as the present owners, the Heywards, point out, extremely labour intensive to care for.

Although the gardens today look as if they have been there for centuries, they were in fact largely the creation of the previous owner, Nancy Lancaster, who restored them in 1955. The original gardens had been neglected, particularly during and after World War II, when the house was requisitioned for use as a prisoner of war camp and as a field hospital. But for the attentions of old Mr Shepherd from the village, who took it upon himself, unasked and unpaid, to keep the

RIGHT A standard honeysuckle (Lonicera periclymenum) marks the corner of a box parterre, which relies for its impact on the contrast between the neatly clipped dark box and the swirling ribbons of the pattern it forms. Where the layout of the parterre is as intricate as this, it pays not to add any further decoration. A simple gravel base is the ideal choice.

topiary chess set in shape during this period, the most striking feature of the gardens, planted in 1850, would have been lost for good. Today it is in pristine condition, diligently tended by the Heywards' current gardeners.

That it does look so immaculate now is the result of a great deal of hard work. When the Heywards took over Haseley Court, the topiary was in need of attention and, as they themselves knew very little about its maintenance, they summoned help from the retired head gardener at Levens Hall (also renowned for its topiary). He spent a considerable amount of time simply shaking dead material out of the hedges, clipping out the dead wood and then applying slow-release fertilizer to encourage new growth. For a couple of years the plants looked embarrassingly 'holey', according to Fiona Heyward, but it was worth it for the magnificent end result.

With topiary, however, the work is never finished: the plants quickly become scruffy unless they are fed regularly and the topiary has to be cut twice a year, in summer and in autumn, to ensure that it never takes on a shaggy appearance. In all there are about 35 clipped pieces in the topiary garden, each of which takes about an hour to cut — by hand — with shears. (According to the Heywards' gardener, electric shears do not give a close enough cut.) It is important to make sure you cut away the new season's growth each time, as it helps to keep the pieces roughly the same size. They do change slowly over about a decade and, at Haseley, some of the larger yews that make a frame for the central chess set are beginning to lean over at a slightly drunken angle. This is because the growth of the trees on one side of the garden has reduced the quantity of light — a problem that the Heywards rectify as best they can by letting the yews grow more bushily on the shady side, while clipping them closer on the side which gets more light.

Although the topiary is very time-consuming, Fiona is adamant that if you are going to have it, it is worth looking after it properly. 'It is essential that it looks well-manicured. You cannot have a sprig out of place.'

BELOW LEFT The art of clipping evergreen shrubs and trees into geometric shapes is known as topiary. It is an art that has been practised in gardens for centuries and provides an opportunity for gardeners to make some kind of personal statement, occasionally a humorous one. One notable piece of topiary has a hunt in full cry sculpted in yew; another has a life-size model of a steam engine.

Yew and box tend to make the best subjects because the foliage is dense and slow-growing, but other evergreens like privet (Ligustrum ovalifolium), holly (Ilex aquifolium) and bay (Laurus nobilis) are also commonly used. For a first attempt at topiary, keep the shape simple — a dome or ball — and clip the plant all over in late summer. It will require regular feeding and watering to keep it in good condition. Use good, sharp shears to clip the plant and start when the plant is young.

Popular shapes include balls, cones, cylinders, spirals and cubes. They look particularly good in matched pairs of containers, flanking paths, arches or doorways.

ABOVE Knot gardens and parterre have been popular since medieval times. Simple geometric patterns of low evergreen hedging plants, they can be created from twisting ribbons of santolina, lavender or box, and infilled with blocks of colour provided by annuals like pelargoniums, marigolds (Tagetes sp), wallflowers, or even bulbs like tulips.

The aim is to form large blocks of colour within the shapes created by the hedges, and to keep the colour scheme restrained — say, blue and gold, or even a single colour such as white.

You must first mark out the design on paper and work out how many small hedging plants will be needed. Most types are planted about 20cm (8in) apart. It is best not to be too ambitious to start with. A front garden would be an ideal place to experiment with a small knot garden — say about 2.2m (7ft) square.

CLIPPING HEDGES

To get a straight outline when clipping an evergreen hedge, such as box or yew, it helps if you tie a length of string to two posts at the height you wish the hedge to be after clipping. You can then use this as a cutting guide to remove the new season's growth. Make sure the shears are really sharp. Take care not to cut through the string!

The topiary is underplanted, parterre-style, with swirling bands of santolina. The aim was to create a thick carpet of it, stretching between the chess pieces, but unfortunately the rabbits have decreed otherwise and have decimated the plants. Replacements are now being grown and the Heywards are trying to deter the marauders by creating a fence of bamboo sticks around each plant. Susan Hampshire suggests that an even more effective remedy is to dip the sticks in renodene (which apparently smells strongly of foxes) and then attach string between the sticks. Although this scares off the rabbits, you have to be careful that the renodene does not touch the plants or their roots as it is poisonous to them.

Nancy Lancaster, now in her nineties, still lives at Haseley, in the Dower House. Under an unusual agreement entered into between her and the Heywards, she has the use of the walled garden, which she created, for her lifetime. According to Fiona Heyward the scheme works surprisingly well. As a result, she has learned a great deal about the gardens and gardening in general from Nancy Lancaster, who in turn has the opportunity to enjoy the garden without all of its attendant responsibilities.

The walled garden is one of the prettiest features of the gardens. Bounded by high stone walls on two sides, and a hornbeam tunnel on the other two, it is divided into quarters. It has paths around the walls and between the quarters, which are lined with apple trees and with standard 'Ballerina' roses, and there is an octagonal gazebo as the central feature. Two of the quarters have lawns edged with box-lined borders; there is a potager in the third quarter, replacing what was once a circular bed of irises and strawberries; and the fourth is a maze-like parterre, the inspiration for which came from the ancient mosaic pavement at Torcello, which Nancy Lancaster saw and admired on

Right The topiary chess set at Haseley is one of the most exquisitely arranged and tended examples in England. It gains its impact not only from the effect of the topiary itself, but from the intricately designed setting. Its curves and neat mounds of santolina and lavender echo the rounded forms of the topiary pieces.

GROWING BOX

This slow-growing evergreen shrub, *Buxus sempervirens*, makes the best low hedge for formal gardens. The species has small, neat, glossy, dark green leaves, which have a distinctive aroma. There are a number of different varieties including *B.s.* 'Elegantissima' which has grey-green leaves edged with silver, and *B.s.* 'Suffruticosa', a dwarf form used for edging.

To propagate box (it is not difficult and is by far the best way to go about creating a hedge) take cuttings about 8cm (3in) long in late summer and, if you have one, insert them in a cold frame, in equal parts of sand and peat. Once the cuttings have rooted, pot them up for a year or so until they are large enough to be planted out to form the hedge.

a visit to Italy. Compartmentalizing a garden is a particularly useful way to approach the design, provided there is some kind of link between the different areas. Screening portions of the garden from each other increases the feeling of space and is a particularly useful device in a smaller garden.

The borders in the walled garden are colour-themed for the seasons, but pink, white and grey predominate. The latter — 'Confederate' grey — is in homage to Nancy Lancaster's background (a Virginian by birth, she is Nancy Astor's niece). The grey has also been used to paint the various seats and is mirrored by the colour of the obelisks that adorn this part of the garden. Old-fashioned perennials like lilies, pinks, stocks, roses and lavenders abound in glorious profusion and, as well as making a splendid counterpoint to the more formal clipped box and standard 'Ballerina' roses, they have the added bonus of creating a wonderfully fragrant potpourri of different scents.

Colour-theming is a useful way of creating unity within a large garden, or even just in a border, and repeating plants has the same harmonizing effect. At Haseley, Fiona uses both of these techniques and also makes good use of clipped box, which provides a frame for so many parts of the garden.

SHRUB ROSES THAT MAKE GOOD STANDARDS

'Ballerina'. Big sprays of small, single pink flowers with a white centre. Mid-green foliage.

'Buff Beauty'. Double flowers in large trusses, from primrose to apricot. Dark green foliage.

'Canary Bird'. Bright yellow single flowers with prominent stamens, well-scented. Dark green almost fern-like foliage.

'The Fairy'. Small pink flowers. Attractive foliage.

'Felicia'. Rich pink double flowers that pale with age. Dark green foliage.

'Nozomi'. Lots of single pearl-pink flowers. Small green leaves.

LEFT To grow a standard, select a healthy plant with a strong single main stem. As the tree grows, remove any side shoots using a sharp pair of secateurs, but leave the side leaves, which are needed to provide food while the plant is still young and growing. When the tree has reached the required height, pinch out the growing tip. If you then wish, clip the plant into shape.

REGALE LILIES

Margery Fish, who gardened at East Lambrook Manor (also open under the National Garden Scheme), was probably one of the best gardeners of her generation. She loved cottage garden flowers, and lilies in particular.

'July is the month when regale lilies scent the air, and their delicious fragrance draws me many times a day to the places where they grow. I don't think it's possible to have too many regale lilies and I plant out every seedling I can find. Seedlings appear all around the plants, sometimes in crevices between stones and in the path. The best regale lilies I have ever seen were growing in an enormous pot, so I put mine in raised beds, tubs and troughs which they have to share with fritillaries, snowdrops and dwarf daffodils. It is a good idea to plant any spare lilies in pots which can be sunk in flower beds needing interest in July.'

(From *A Flower for Every Day*, Faber, 1981.)

COMPANION PLANTS FOR ROSES

The leggy stems of roses are often best disguised with other plants. Meriel Toynbee used campanulas very successfully (see pp. 46-9). Other good plants are lavender and catmint, with its feathery, silvery foliage and soft blue flowers. Margery Fish recommends hostas. 'A small rose garden had the climbing rose "New Dawn" trained on one side. It was to make a screen and, all along the bottom, these magnificent hostas were growing. The very pale pink of the roses was entrancingly lovely with the leaves of the hosta and its pale lilac flowers.'

Lilies are among Fiona Heyward's favourite plants, along with old-fashioned roses, and she often plants them in containers. The big, intoxicatingly-scented regale lilies are particular favourites, and remarkably easy to grow. The funnel-shaped white waxy flowers, up to 12cm (5in) long, are borne in loose clusters in midsummer. An added boon is that they will increase quite quickly if planted in good soil and full sun. If you want to grow them in pots, put about three bulbs in a 25cm (10in) pot in autumn, planted fairly deep in good potting compost.

One of the most attractive features of the garden is the variety of design and planting. Two of the ten acres are devoted to woodland, fortunately so, perhaps, as it is less labour-intensive than the herbaceous borders and the potager. The nut trees in the wood are underplanted with a mass of spring bulbs — daffodils, snowdrops, *Anemone blanda* and fritillaries among them — and the attractive drooping flowers of *Helleborus orientalis*. There are also Turk's cap lilies (*Lilium martagon*), which have colonized remarkably well. Handsome plants, about 1.4m (5ft) tall, the species has spires of rose-purple flowers in midsummer. There is also a white form, *L.m. alba*.

One of the changes made by the Heywards was to remove a double avenue of dying chestnuts at the front of the house and replace them with an even longer avenue of limes. Planted around four years ago, these already make an impact, stretching away into the distance from the terrace of Haseley Court.

As well as everything else, there is a handsome water feature at Haseley, in the shape of a formal canal and connecting pools, created in the eighteenth century. Today it is home to water birds and to a large colony of carp.

TOWN GARDEN
25 ELLESMERE ROAD

THIS COULD WELL BE DESCRIBED as a foliage garden. It makes a wonderfully rich tapestry of green, in which form and structure play as important a role as colour, and, to create it, a wide range of contrasting plant forms, leaf shapes and textures have been used. The garden is relatively small — approximately 18m x 22m (60 x 70ft) — and Penny Sinclair feels that too many bright colours are best avoided in such a small space.

One of the reasons why Penny Sinclair has opted for a wide variety of foliage plants is that flowering is very unreliable in the English climate. Foliage is, therefore, a far sounder bet. The other problem, she says, in a small garden is that you cannot hide the remnants of dying flower heads easily, so it is better to focus attention on plants that have a more permanent quality.

Although she does not favour any specific plants, Penny has certain preferences, and deliberately repeats these plants around the garden. It helps to give a small garden a feeling of unity and avoid the

HOSTAS FOR THE GARDEN

Hostas leaves will scorch and curl up in strong sunlight, so make sure they are provided with a bit of shade, whether they are planted directly into the soil or into pots.

Hosta fortunei has large handsome leaves about 23cm (9in) long, and does best in deep moist soil and some shade. A variety, *H.f.* 'Aurea' has butter-yellow leaves that go greener as they age, and there is also a cream and green variegated one called. *H.f.* 'Marginata Alba'.

H. sieboldiana is the species with the largest leaves of all the hostas, about 30cm (12in) long, and lilac flower heads. The variety *H.s.* 'Elegans' has particularly handsome large waxy blue leaves.

H. tardiana 'Halcyon' is probably the bluest of the blue-leaved hostas, although smaller than *H.s.* 'Elegans'.

LEFT A rich contrast of shape and texture in the front garden illustrates the charm of Penny Sinclair's planting. Large floppy evergreen bergenia leaves contrast with the formality of the clipped yew and box.

ABOVE In the front garden at 25 Ellesmere Road, the garden gate has been painted to echo the soft bluish-grey tones of the Jackman's blue rue. Neatly clipped yew and box contrast with the softly billowing mounds of rue and the swathes of wisteria over the front door, whose purple paint makes a perfect foil for the group of bright pink busy lizzies and grey-green hosta leaves by the doorstep.

spotty, restless look that a garden with too many clashing flower colours tends to have. She uses a lot of evergreen shrubs, both as dividers for the sections of the garden and as a backdrop to the more ephemeral planting. Laurel, pyracantha, privet, yew and box feature prominently, the latter two clipped neatly into hedges where appropriate. Ivies also appear frequently around the garden. There is a wide range to choose from, with a surprising variety of leaf shape and colour, from the variegated leaves of 'Paddy's Pride (correctly, *Hedera colchicha* 'Poetica') to the neat arrow-shaped foliage of *H.h.* 'Sagittifolia' and the golden-splashed forms.

The front garden is designed on formal lines, with a central cross created by the brick paths, bounded on each side by low clipped box hedges and pyramids of clipped box and yew at the corners. Plants with a sprawling habit, such as the blue rue (*Ruta graveolens* 'Jackman's Blue') have been chosen as a counterpoint to the formality and neatness of the geometric shapes of the box and the brick, and the effect is both dramatic and satisfying. This is further enhanced by the contrast in forms — sharp spires of sisyrinchium mingle with soft mounds of senecios and bergenias. Such patterns and colours are repeated in the other two parts of the garden — the side and back — and help give an overall feeling of unity.

The back garden is laid out as a town garden, with a rectangle of beautifully kept grass ('I sit in a deckchair in the summer', says Penny, 'and dig the weeds out by hand with a screwdriver.'), paved areas and shrub borders. The garden appears much larger than it actually is as a result of Penny's strategy of making separate rooms, screened from each other by large evergreen shrubs. One of the most distinctive features of the garden is the meticulous attention to detail, right down to the carefully selected colours of the garden gates. They are painted in subtle shades of duck-egg blue and sage green, deliberately chosen to echo the colours of the foliage. The front door of the house, painted an arresting deep purple, makes a pool of colour at the end of the front path as you enter the garden, in contrast to the quiet greens and greys of the foliage.

GROWING HOSTAS IN POTS

The natural vase shape of the hosta makes it a very fitting subject for a terracotta pot. As hostas are notoriously susceptible to slug damage (left untreated their leaves will rapidly turn into an interesting but unattractive filigree of veins, the juicier parts completely eaten away), it is a good idea to grow them in pots. You can then spread very sharp grit not only over the surface of the compost in the pot, but over the area surrounding the base of the pot as well. Few slugs or snails will brave this equivalent of a fakir's bed of nails. According to Beth Chatto, bark chippings will do a similar job in borders.

Plant the hosta in a good size pot – at least 25cm (10in) in diameter – and fill the base with broken clay pots for drainage. Using good potting compost, plant the hosta, firm it in and water well. Do not stand hostas in full sun or the leaves will scorch.

GOOD EVERGREENS

There are a number of good evergreens to make a structural framework for a foliage garden. Among them are:

Ivy *(Hedera)*. You will find a wide variety of forms of ivy, most of them self-clinging. They are particularly useful for growing in shade, although the variegated forms need some light. Some of the better known ones include *Hedera helix* 'Goldheart' with gold centres to the leaves, *H.h.* 'Sagittifolia' with arrow-shaped dark green leaves, and *H. canariensis* 'Gloire de Marengo' with silver-variegated foliage.

Box *(Buxus sempervirens)*. See p.14

Yew *(Taxus baccata)*. A slow-growing conifer, yew is a wonderful plant for clipping and for providing a backdrop to a border. If not clipped, it will eventually grow to around 15m (50ft). There are several varieties, some with golden-variegated foliage.

Christmas box, Sweet box *(Sarcococca)*. Not to be confused with ordinary box, *Sarcococca* has glossy dark green leaves and deliciously scented white flowers in winter, followed by black fruits. One species, *S. confusa*, is a bit smaller than the other, *S. hookeriana*, which grows to about 1.4m (5ft) tall and wide.

Laurel *(Prunus)*. There are several different forms of laurel, but one of the most attractive is *Prunus laurocerasus* 'Otto Luyken', which has wonderfully shiny, dark green leaves. In late spring these are held slightly aloft, with spikes of white flowers. Cherry red fruits follow. It grows to a height of about 1.2m (4ft), and about the same width.

Aucuba japonica. A bushy shrub with large leaves, it reaches a height of 2.5m (8ft). There is a variety with gold-splashed leaves, called 'Crotonifolia'. Bright red berries follow the rather insignificant flowers.

ABOVE A cheap way to simulate a Gothic wrought-iron coping is to glue together plastic lawn edging with a strong all-purpose adhesive and then paint it with two or three coats of matt black external use paint.

With great panache, Penny has given the glass house adjoining her home an authentic Victorian look by the addition of a gable created from plastic lawn edging, glued back to back, and painted black. Costing a fraction of the real thing, it is guaranteed to fool anyone.

Large-leaved foliage plants in terracotta pots furnish the patio in the back garden. The large handsome waxy leaves and tall white flower spires of *Hosta sieboldiana* 'Elegans' make a particularly striking display. Hostas are among her favourite pot-grown subjects, and she prefers to keep the containers simple, sometimes limiting herself to just a single species of plant in each. Other possibilities for containers, in use at Ellesmere Road, are parsley, which makes an excellent foil for bright-coloured annuals, and oak-leaved lettuce with its russet-coloured indented leaves.

Beautifully maintained, the garden at Ellesmere Road is a model of how to garden in the limited space afforded by a town garden, with a real sense of elegance and style. As Penny says, it is not a plantsman's garden because she does not grow a great range of unusual plants; it is, however, very sympathetically planted and blends beautifully with the architecture of the house.

VEGETABLE GARDEN
THE CROFT

GROWING PEARS

Growing pears as espaliers against a wall is a good method of ensuring a successful crop, as the trees greatly benefit from the shelter the wall gives them from the wind. Espalier pears are normally planted at about four years old and start bearing fruit the next year. The leading shoots are trained out horizontally to the left and right, along wires which have been attached to the wall for this purpose.

Remember that pears need to have a pollinator to bear fruit, so always grow two of them.

LEFT Brassicas in one of the triangular beds, with pears grown espalier-style on the brick walls behind. The soil at The Croft is naturally flinty and requires a lot of organic matter to be added to produce good crops like these.

RIGHT An old sundial forms the central feature of the ornamental potager, seen here with one of the herb and strawberry beds behind. Gravel paths divide the beds, which are neatly edged with bricks.

S USAN HAMPSHIRE IS NOT ALONE in her passion for freshly picked home-grown vegetables. Few gardens give a better opportunity to indulge in this passion than the Carvers' garden at The Croft, where there is a huge walled vegetable garden, laid out in the ornamental style that earns it the name 'potager'.

The soft red brick walls and yew hedges provide the necessary shelter for a wide range of vegetables, herbs and fruit, laid out in a design that features four central triangular beds divided by two diagonal gravel paths with a stone sundial in the middle where they cross. Clipped box cones stand sentinel at the outer corners of the beds and the triangular theme is echoed by both the portico over the door to the garden and the handsome cloches under which some of the early vegetables are forced. Rectangular beds run alongside the

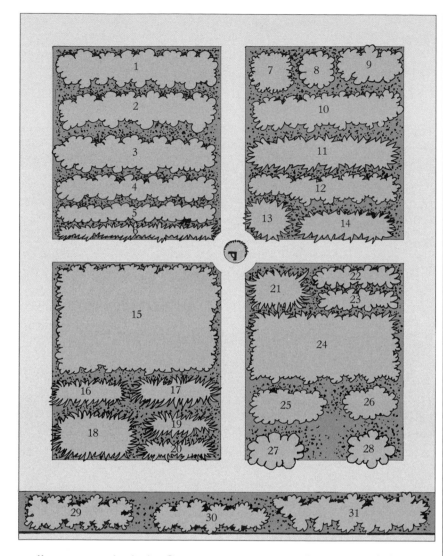

Left This is an outline plan for a vegetable garden, divided by paths into four main blocks, with a central sundial and a fifth bed underneath a wall at the bottom. Clipped box at the corners of the beds, herbs as edgings and brick or gravel paths will make it more ornamental, as will the addition of gooseberries grown as standards at the corners and climbing plants on the walls or fences around it.

The key is as follows: 1 Spring cabbages, 2 Cauliflowers, 3 Calabrese, 4 Brussels sprouts, 5 Purple-sprouting broccoli, 6 Spinach, 7 Lamb's lettuce, 8 Oak-leaved and salad bowl lettuce, 9 Purslane, 10 Broad beans, 11 Dwarf French beans, 12 Peas, 13 and 14 Runner beans (wigwam and row), 15 Potatoes, 16 Leeks for autumn, 17 Leeks for winter, 18 Onions, 19 Spring onions, 20 Garlic, 21 Beetroot, 22 Parsnips, 23 Celeriac, 24 Strawberries, 25 and 26 Courgettes, 27 and 28 Rhubarb, 29 Tomatoes, 30 and 31 Fruit canes and bushes.

walls, against which the Carvers grow a range of ornamental climbers — principally roses and clematis — as well as espaliered fruit trees.

The ability to grow good vegetables depends, as Jacky Carver points out, on the quality of the soil. Since their own soil is very light, free-draining and full of stones and flints, they add considerable quantities of organic matter to the soil, principally in the form of mushroom compost. In a light soil like that of The Croft, it is vitally important to add moisture-retaining matter to get good crops of runner beans. Failure to do so will result in dry, stringy pods. The Carvers dig a deep trench in the early spring and line it with organic matter and mushroom compost, but even old newspapers will do the job just as well.

The Carvers' vegetables are a testament to the success of their soil improvement programme; they boast excellent crops of asparagus,

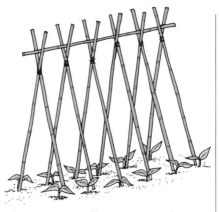

courgettes, brassicas, runner beans, potatoes, carrots and many more. As the Carvers point out, if you are going to spend a lot of time growing vegetables, it makes sense to grow the best, and to grow some of the varieties less commonly available in the shops.

Another important factor in vegetable growing is to rotate the crops; in other words, not to grow the same crops in the same place several years running. Rotation, as even medieval peasants realized, helps to cut down on pests and diseases, and prevents soil sickness. When planning a new vegetable garden and attempting to clear the ground, potatoes make an excellent first crop, as they help to break up the soil. Then, a normal, yearly rotation plan for a small vegetable garden could be: plot A, potatoes; plot B, brassicas; plot C, peas and beans; plot D, root crops.

Protection from frost is important for early crops. In addition to their classically shaped cloches, the Carvers use fleece as a cover for their young carrots. It is not the most attractive sight, but it certainly does the job efficiently. The Carvers are adamant that vegetables should be picked when they are young and tender, particularly in the case of carrots and courgettes. If they are not needed immediately the carrots can simply be stored in sand for later use.

In addition to the vegetable garden, The Croft has some fine parkland, with magnificent trees. Part of it is devoted to a handsome, formal 'tapis vert', an area of grass mown into geometric patterns, with statues positioned at strategic points. Something similar could be created on a much smaller scale in a town garden. Another theme in the Carvers' garden is that they have marked various family occasions with special additions to the garden — a pavilion for their son's twenty-first birthday, a rose walk for their twenty-fifth wedding anniversary and a little temple for Peter Carver's fiftieth birthday.

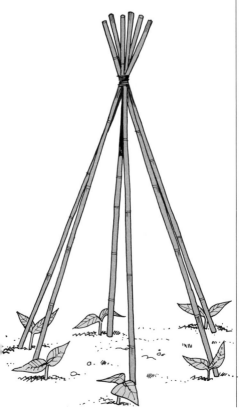

ABOVE AND BELOW To grow runner beans, dig a deep trench — at least two spades deep — and line it with well-rotted vegetable matter or old newspapers to help retain the moisture before backfilling it. Then plant the beans after all danger of frost has passed. Next make a framework of canes, one for each bean plant, either tied together at the top to form a cross, or made to form a circular wigwam shape which can look very decorative.

ALTERNATIVE SALAD VEGETABLES

All these salad vegetables can be grown using the 'cut and come again' method, by which the plant will resprout if the leaves are only harvested from the plant's neck.

Corn salad (lamb's lettuce). A good substitute for lettuce, it can be sown in *situ* and should be repeatedly thinned out from spring to autumn, to about 10cm (4in) apart. Protect it with cloches in winter. The thinned-out seedlings can be used as greenery in salads.

Salad bowl (oak-leaved lettuce).

These can be grown very close together and harvested like corn salad. Sow the seed broadcast in *situ*. The plants — particularly the russet-coloured forms — can be used as edging for a bed in a potager, as they are very ornamental.

Purslane. This needs full sun, shelter and well-drained soil. Sow in succession from May to June in the open and thin to about 15cm (6in) apart. Successional sowings will produce crops until autumn.

NEW GARDEN
STAR COTTAGE

———— •• • ————

I T IS A MOOT POINT whether it is easier to renovate an existing garden or
to start from scratch on a bare plot. Lys de Bray, a well-known
botanical illustrator and gardening writer, took on the challenge of the
latter at Star Cottage.

As a painter, Lys is well used to being confronted with a blank
canvas, so she found the experience less daunting than most would
have done. She also had the added advantage of being able to transfer
a large number of well-grown plants from her previous garden, which
helped her establish her new garden relatively easily.

However, if you start, as she did, from nothing, you must have a
very clear idea of what you want. Lys drew up a proper plan on paper
— an essential element, she feels, in planning any new garden —

*BELOW The Victorian urn that forms the centrepiece of Lys de Bray's arbour has
begonias and ageratum planted around its base. The urn itself plays host to
miniature pink roses and silver-leaved helichrysum.*

LYCHNIS CORONARIA

• •

The deep magenta blooms of *Lychnis coronaria* make a striking feature in any border. A clump-forming perennial, it grows to about 45–60cm (18–24in) high. It has small grey leaves and brilliant flowers, which are held aloft in panicles on silvery stems. (There is also a white form known as *L. c. alba*.)

Provided that it is planted both in a sunny position and in well-drained soil, it self seeds easily.

LEFT It is hard to believe that this photograph was taken when the garden was less than one year old. It demonstrates just what an achievement it was to move so many plants and create what is — in effect — an instant garden. To see similar sleights of hand you normally have to visit the Chelsea Flower Show.

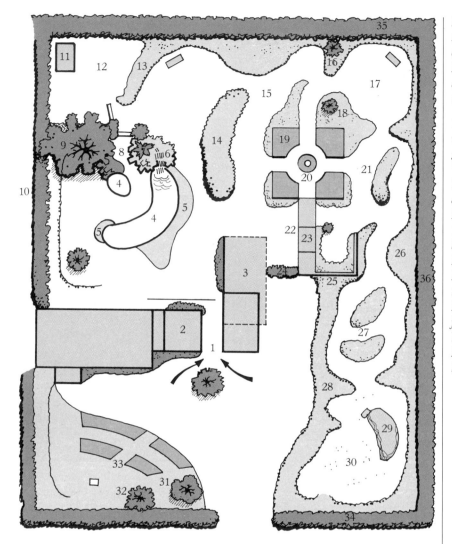

LEFT When planning a garden, you should draw in the major features in scale on a plan. The plan here is of Lys de Bray's garden. Once you have organized a sound framework, you can start to plan the planting in detail.

1 *Garden entrance,* 2 *Studio,* 3 *Proposed new studio and gallery,* 4 *Pond,* 5 *Bog garden,* 6 *Waterfall,* 7 *Cedrus atlantica 'Glauca',* 8 *Rockery,* 9 *Fernery,* 10 *Eucalyptus gunnii,* 11 *and* 12 *Pottering and sitting area,* 13 *Grasses,* 14 *Herbaceous border,* 15 *Autumn garden,* 16 *Arbutus unedo,* 17 *Glade,* 18 *Shakespeare's oak,* 19 *Old roses,* 20 *Formal garden,* 21 *Winter garden,* 22 *Roses,* 23 *Pergola,* 24 *Hedge,* 25 *Wall,* 26 *Spring garden,* 27 *Foliage garden,* 28 *Flowering shrubs,* 29 *Dinosaur's footprint rock,* 30 *Wild flower lawn,* 31 *Rhus typhina,* 32 *Syringa vulgaris,* 33 *Modern roses,* 34 *Laid hedge,* 35 *Native hedge,* 36 *Tapestry hedge.*

although she has not stuck to it to the letter in the actual planting. Borders and gardens change constantly, both throughout the seasons and over the years, and it never pays to be inflexible. She has several different borders in the garden, all themed in a specific way, including a double herbaceous border, which was meticulously planned on paper, with flowering times, colours and heights all carefully charted. But even the best-designed plans go awry. Not all the plants are what they purport to be and, in one instance, Lys ended up with a particularly unwelcome combination of a creamy poppy with a very pale lilac mallow, when the intention had been to stick to shades of white and cream in this part of the border.

A very useful tip that Lys offers is to keep a garden book in which to note down exactly when and where each plant flowers, and the combinations of plants that work well together, so that you can repeat

---

UNUSUAL CLIMBERS FOR ARBOURS

Aristolochia macrophylla. Also known as Dutchman's pipe, after the shape of its flowers, this is predominantly a foliage plant, with handsome, large heart-shaped leaves and yellow, brown and green flowers which appear in early summer. It will grow to about 6m (20ft) in sun or shade.

Campsis radicans. Also known as the trumpet vine, this self-clinging climber has orange, trumpet-shaped flowers and feathery, divided leaves. It needs full sun and a very warm site, as it is only half-hardy. Given the right conditions it can grow to a height of 12m (40ft).

Passiflora caerulea. Also known as passion flower, this strong-growing climber — it can reach a height of 6m (12ft) — has beautiful round bluish-white flowers with prominent stamens. In a hot summer it will also produce fruit.

Solanum crispum 'Glasnevin'. This variety of the Chilean potato tree is hardier than the rest of the species, and semi-evergreen. It has purple flowers for a long season in summer and will grow to about 4.5m (15ft). Another species, *Solanum jasminoides,* is evergreen but less hardy. It has pale blue flowers, while *S.j.* 'Album' has white flowers.

BELOW Arbours come in many different forms, but whichever type you choose, it is essential that it is securely anchored into the ground. Otherwise, the combined weight of the arbour and the climbing plants covering it will almost certainly bring the whole edifice down in high winds.

The supporting posts should be sunk into the ground and set in concrete, the depth depending on the height of the arbour. Ask your garden centre for instructions at the time of purchase.

them if you wish. Knowing what you have planted, and where, is very helpful in a new garden, as it is all to easy to dig up one of your prized possessions in the spring before it has come into new growth. Losing valued plants is a great sadness to all gardeners, especially when it is through your own carelessness.

Lys's quarter-acre garden includes many striking features, not least a large Victorian urn of which she is inordinately fond. Its rather grand nature dictated a formal setting, so Lys created an arbour, with a trellis as a backdrop. Over this trellis she is now growing several climbers, including *Clematis montana* 'Grandiflora Alba', several old-fashioned roses, a pink *Stephanotis* and a variegated morning glory (*Ipomoea sp*). Around the base she has planted wallflowers and nasturtiums, mixed with small sunflowers. Any large-scale architectural element in the garden, such as an arbour, needs careful planning to avoid costly mistakes. The other large feature is an ornamental pool, and Lys called in professionals to help with the landscaping.

New gardens, particularly those on brand new estates, suffer greatly from a lack of shelter. Very few plants take kindly to exposure from cold winds, and one of the first considerations in planting up any new garden is to create some form of shelter belt, either with fencing or with shrubs and trees. Along one side of her garden, Lys is planning to plant hollies and Portuguese laurels, while among the trees on another boundary, she is already growing large scrambling roses, such as 'Paul's Himalayan Musk', 'Bobbie James', 'Kiftsgate' and 'Frances E. Lester', that will happily scale any trees in their vicinity.

HERB GARDEN
THE COTTAGE HERBERY

Tthe popularity of herbs has greatly increased as people have grown more aware of their culinary and medicinal potential. For Kim Hurst and her husband Rob they have become a way of life. Indeed Kim has gradually allowed her interest in herbs to turn into a full-scale business.

Kim and Rob first became interested in herbs when Rob, now a hop farmer (and hops, incidentally, are herbs as well), was at Agricultural College in Shropshire. Nearby there were two good herb gardens that they visited frequently, and their enthusiasm started there, fostered by Barbara Keen, whose garden at Valeswood was a major source of inspiration to them at the time.

Kim has spent a lot of time studying the work of herbalists like Nicholas Culpepper and the herb garden is designed, in part, around

GOOD KING HENRY

This herb gives really good value and can be used as a vegetable like spinach. You can grow good King Henry (*Chenopodium bonus-henricus*) from seed sown indoors in spring, pricked out and then planted out in late spring about 35cm (14in) apart. Use the leaves in the first season and the stems in the second. Once you have established a bed of plants, you can divide them to create more.

Left A lion mask is half hidden in a surrounding mass of herbs. A hop (Humulus lupulus) *climbs behind the head of the statue, and there are two forms of elder* (Sambucus) *in the background, including the golden variegated form 'Aureomarginata'. Goat's rue* (Galega officinalis), *lungworts* (Pulmonaria sp), *comfrey* (Symphytum) *and avens* (Geum) *form the bulk of the underplanting.*

LEFT A group of variegated leaved herbs in which the large, white-splashed leaves of pulmonaria make a handsome clump. These are surrounded by larnium and backed by hardy geraniums.

BELOW An orange-flowered lily makes a vivid contrast in this herb bed, which is dominated by the purple-leaved sage, Salvia officinalis 'Purpurascens'. Also present are chives, orach and marjoram.

THE ASTROLOGICAL GARDEN

The Hursts' astrological garden is based on the writings of Nicholas Culpepper, the famous seventeenth-century herbalist who used the astrological signs and the planets to help treat his patients.

Culpepper was born on 18 October 1616 (a Libran) and at the age of 24 set himself up as a doctor and apothecary in a large house next to the Red Lion Inn in Spitalfields, in London's East End. An anti-royalist, he fought at the Battle of Edge Hill in 1642, where he received a serious chest wound and later contracted tuberculosis. Although he never totally recovered his health, he lived on until 1654 and wrote many books, including his renowned *Complete Herbal*, which is still on sale today.

The design of the garden, a circle divided into twelve equal parts, mirrors that of an astrological chart. The herbs have then been planted in accordance with their association with each of the twelve star signs. People who were born under the star sign of Leo, for example, are supposed to suffer from ailments in their heart, spine and lower arms, and, for Leos, the herbs that should be used to treat these conditions are angelica, bay, borage, marigold, motherwort, peony and rue.

This key lists first the ailments which particularly afflict people born under each star sign and then the herbs most suited to treat these ailments, which are planted in their respective segments of the circle.

Aries: head.
Sweet marjoram, rosemary, horseradish, cowslip, betony and garlic.

Taurus: neck and throat.
Garden mint, thyme, coltsfoot and lovage.

Gemini: hands, arms and lungs.
Lavender, parsley, caraway and dill.

Cancer: breasts and stomach.
Honeysuckle, loosestrife, hyssop and balm.

Leo: heart, spine and lower arms.
Motherwort, angelica, marigold, rue, bay, borage and peony.

Virgo: abdomen, hands and intestines.
Southernwood, valerians, fennel and savory.

Libra: lower back and kidneys.
Marshmallow, pennyroyal, mugwort and yarrow.

Scorpio: pelvis and sex organs.
Tarragon, wormwood and basil.

Sagittarius: hips, thighs and liver.
Houseleek, chervil and sage.

Capricorn: knees and bones.
Solomon's seal, comfrey and sorrel.

Aquarius: shins and ankles.
Elderberry, mullein and bistort.

Pisces: feet.
Meadowsweet, lungwort and agrimony.

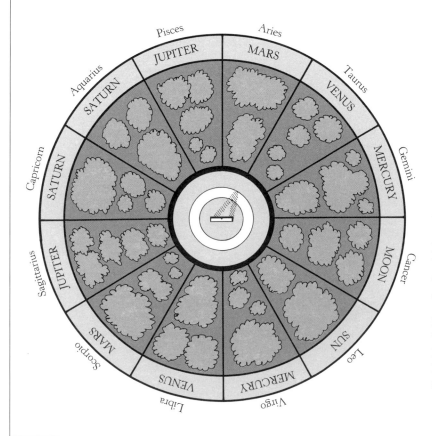

GOOD KING HENRY AND HOP SHOOT FLAN

220g (8oz) of wholemeal pastry
10 small Good King Henry leaves
thyme, chopped
2 large eggs
1 large onion, diced
10 hop shoots
175g (6oz) mature cheddar, grated
Sesame seed

Make pastry as you would
normally, roll out and line an 8in
(20cm) flan dish. Bake blind. Beat

eggs. Chop up Good King Henry
leaves and add with the thyme to
the beaten eggs. Put the onion and
hop shoots into the pastry case and
gently pour on the herb and egg
mix. Sprinkle on the cheese, then
finish with the sesame seed. Place in
a preheated oven at 220° C (425°F,
Mark 7) for 15 minutes. Lower
heat to 180°C (350°F, Mark 4) for a
further 20 minutes until golden
brown. Serve either hot or cold.

BELOW Herbs smell absolutely delicious, none more so than myrtle (Myrtus communis) which makes the centrepiece of one of Kim's pots. Its small evergreen leaves are wonderfully aromatic, as are its delicate creamy flowers. Around it plant purple-flowered lemon thyme (Thymus x citriodorus), creeping savory (Satureia montana subspicata) with its tiny white flowers and tricoloured sage (Salvia officinalis 'Tricolor').

some of Culpepper's ideas and theories. As a result the herbs at the Cottage Herbery are organized in various themed beds. One bed, for example, has been turned into an astrological and medicinal bed. Culpepper believed that for every star sign of the zodiac there were appropriate herbal remedies for the ailments that each person was particularly prone to. Susan Hampshire, as a Taurean, should be susceptible to throat infections (true, she says!), and infusions of thyme are purported to help ward these off and alleviate the symptoms when the infection develops.

Kim goes to a herbalist herself and is insistent that it is not a good idea to treat yourself, although it does no harm to use herbal remedies for minor ailments.

There is also a culinary herb bed in the garden, with all the best pot herbs, a 'bee and tea' bed, with herbs for attracting bees and for making infusions, and an aromatic herb bed. On the drawing board for next year are a Chinese medicinal herb garden and a dye plant garden.

The gardens are about one acre in total, with about half of this devoted to the herb beds and one quarter to a wild garden. The remaining quarter acre is laid out as a cottage garden, where the plants include some of the rarer herbs. Kim and Rob also make collections of individual species, like comfreys (*Symphytum*), lungworts (*Pulmonaria*) and astrantias.

Kim and Rob garden organically and they now use their own form of coir compost which they actually market under the name of 'Fertile Fibre'. It certainly seems to work very well as they won a Silver Medal at the Chelsea Flower Show in 1992, the first time that they had not only exhibited at the show, but ever been there. They visit quite a few shows round the country — a major element in their herb business — and have won awards elsewhere as well.

GARDEN ROOMS
TURN END

· • ·

A<small>S IS THE CASE WITH</small> many of the gardens featured in this book, the Aldingtons were confronted with a wilderness when they first moved to Turn End. They were fortunate in that, in time, the bones of a former garden emerged from beneath the undergrowth. Today, however, the garden is rather larger than it was originally as, over the years, the Aldingtons have added to their land. As a result, the garden now comprises a series of compartments and the Aldingtons have cleverly managed to turn this to their advantage. Each compartment has a different theme, which has enabled them to blend the formal with the informal and to indulge in a wide variety of planting. In addition, as you approach each separate part, you get a tantalizing glimpse of what is in store, through archways, arbours and carefully contrived gaps in the planting.

The immediate lesson that Turn End has for an aspiring gardener is that a garden's charm is greatly increased if you are unable to see all parts of it at once. Each corner turned presents an exciting new vista

YUCCA

· • ·

Planted in tall containers, yuccas make an ideal focal point in a garden, with their striking rosettes of sword-shaped leaves. When they flower, they produce a single massive spire up to 2.5m (8ft) high of bells in various shades of white. All species of *Yucca*, of which *Y. gloriosa* is the biggest, are evergreen and have spiny leaves. *Y. recurvifolia* differs in that its older leaves tend to curve downwards and its flower spike is not quite as tall.

L<small>EFT</small> *In this corner of the Mediterranean garden are a series of troughs and containers holding just a few of the Aldingtons' impressive collection of alpine plants.*

R<small>IGHT</small> *One of the many intriguing views at Turn End, offering a hint of what lies around the next corner. Clematis and roses adorn the pergola, which provides a link between the sunken garden and the lawned area beyond.*

and also helps make the garden appear far larger than it actually is. In many ways it is the ideal garden to visit as it has something for everyone. It is especially worth seeing if you are a novice gardener, trying to find out what plants you like and what style of garden you want.

By one corner of the house there is a small courtyard with a cool, shady pond, while by another is a mini woodland garden full of spring bulbs. In the woodland garden, there is a small grove of birch trees planted close to the house. Most gardening books suggest that trees should be planted at the further end of the garden, but the Aldingtons have deliberately broken the rules both in the woodland area and by the pond. In the case of Turn End this is most effective, as it prevents you from seeing all of the garden from the house and so increases the feeling of surprise and secrecy. Birches, such as *Betula alba septentrionalis* and *B. utilis jaquemontii*, with their attractive papery silver bark and graceful slender trunks, are particularly suited to achieving this end as, although they impede the view, they never actually obscure it completely.

Nearby is a hot and sunny walled garden with raised beds and, further from the house, are herbaceous borders, a tiny, paved daisy garden, a formal parterre and another courtyard with a multitude of shrubs and climbers.

The little courtyard close to the house has been designed so as to join the garden and house into a seamless unit. Peter Aldington, an architect, designed the house himself and this small courtyard, divided from the house by large picture windows, immediately brings a feeling of peace and spaciousness into the house, while providing a bridge between the architecture of the house and the planting beyond.

LEFT Most woody shrubs and some herbaceous plants, particularly carnations and pinks, can be increased by layering in the autumn. Find a healthy shoot that is long enough to reach the ground easily, remove some of the leaves, and make a small cut with a sharp knife (to encourage rooting) at the point where it can be pegged down in the soil. Keep it in position with a U pin or with stones, and cover with compost until rooted. Don't be impatient — it takes a long time.

The pond is quite shady and as a result lacks enough light for water-lilies to grow well, so the water hawthorn, *Aponogeton distachyos*, has been planted instead. Like water-lilies, the water hawthorn's flowers are waxy and white and the leaves, although long, elegant and spear-shaped rather than round, float similarly on the water. There the similarity ends, as the water hawthorn has clusters of small white bell-like flowers, which are heavily scented and have a particularly long flowering season.

The herbaceous borders that surround the lawned area behind the house are attractively relaxed. In planting their borders, the Aldingtons concentrate not only colour but also on form. They use interesting verticals, such as tall thistles (*Onopordium acanthium*), which grow to a height of about 2m (6ft) and produce attractive pale lilac flowers above the rosettes of silvery spiny leaves, and foxgloves, adding yet further to the architecture of their perennial planting. Both these plants self-seed easily in the right conditions

A magnificent terracotta pot by Monica Young makes a focal point in the shadier part of the border, surrounded by handsome foliage plants — ferns, ligularias and peltiphyllums — which thrive in these conditions. Irises also make good architectural plants, their clumps of strap-shaped leaves creating an interesting counterpoint to more mound-forming perennials like hardy geraniums. The Aldingtons have quite a collection of irises, which can be found in a wonderful range of colours and for almost every kind of situation — from tiny reticulatas for the rock garden to the big bearded irises for the borders.

ABOVE Many bulbs, such as narcissi, produce small offsets at the base of the bulb. These can be removed after the bulbs have flowered and the leaves have died down, and then grown on in pots in good cuttings compost or in a nursery bed. When they have reached flowering size they can be planted out in their proper places.

HELLEBORES

Hellebores are something of an acquired taste. Novice gardeners tend to be attracted by either quantities of blossom or large bright flowers and would probably overlook hellebores in the garden centre. They do however possess hidden charms — you have to stoop down and lift their flower heads to appreciate the true quality of their very delicate, and often beautifully marked, flowers. Certain species have the added advantage of evergreen leaves. Some hellebores are quite promiscuous and will interbreed easily, producing interesting variations in any collection you may acquire.

The flowers vary in colour according to the species, or to the hybrids. The white Christmas rose (*Helleborus niger*) is well known because it blooms, unusually, in the winter. The Lenten rose, *H. orientalis*, blooms, as you might guess, in early spring, with flowers in crimson, cream, purple and pink, variously freckled and spotted. Good for borders is the larger *H. corsicus*, with its handsome evergreen leaves and smaller yellowish green flowers. *H. guttatus*, a parent of many dark maroonish black hybrids, like 'Prince Rupert', has attractively speckled flowers.

In Edwardian times, it was fashionable to plant specialized iris beds, but most gardeners today, like the Aldingtons, prefer to incorporate them with other plants in a mixed border.

As the borders approach the woodland garden, there are a multitude of spring flowers, like wallflowers and tulips, and tall, handsome, summer-flowering irises, foxgloves, poppies and alliums.

The alliums also make an exciting combination with the 'Cerise Bouquet' rose that overhangs a path in the woodland garden. One of the most handsome plants in the onion family, *Allium christophii* has huge globe-like heads of tiny, starry, mauve flowers. Not only do the flower heads last a long time, but they then fade into attractive straw-coloured seed heads which are well worth picking for the house. *A. christophii*, which can be propagated from the offsets it freely produces, flowers in June on stems about 90cm (3ft) tall. It may need staking in a windy site and, although it prefers full sun, it will tolerate some shade, as here next to the 'Cerise Bouquet' rose. The latter is a

RIGHT In any well-designed border, foliage is as important as flower colour. Here, large variegated hosta leaves have created an almost luminous effect against a dark green backdrop of ferns, ligularias, pulmonarias and astilbes.

ARCHITECTURAL PLANTS

Cynara cardunculus. Also known as the cardoon, this makes a splendid feature plant with its arching silvery grey leaves and large heads of blue thistle-like flowers. It grows to 2m (6ft) tall, and does best in full sun.

Eryngium giganteum. Known as Miss Willmott's Ghost after the Edwardian gardener who used to walk around people's gardens spreading its seed, this handsome plant has branching heads of metallic-looking leaves and blue-green flowers. Prefers full sun, where it will grow to about 75cm (2½ft).

Melianthus major. This tall-growing plant has large silvery-green toothed leaves and spikes of brownish red flowers in spring to summer. It does best in the sun and well-drained soil and grows to about 2.2m (7ft).

Rheum palmatum. The ornamental rhubarb makes a wide-spreading mound of massive hand-shaped leaves, with reddish stems, and undersides, and a spire up to 2.4m (8ft) high of creamy flowers in summer. It needs good, moist soil and some sun.

Veratrum album. The false hellebore, as it is sometimes called, grows to 1.5 to 2m (5 to 6ft) tall, with large leaves that are pleated rather like a fan. In late summer, it produces a tall flower stem of small white flowers. It does well in retentive soil and will cope with partial shade.

Verbascum. There are several forms of mullein, but the largest species is *V. olympicum*, which grows to about 2m (6ft). It has soft-felted, silvery grey foliage and tall spires of golden flowers in summer.

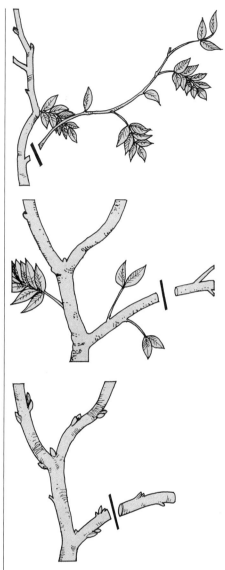

ABOVE A wisteria should be pruned twice a year. In the summer, the long shoots (1) and lateral growths (2) should be cut back to encourage flowering (a few leaves should be left on the shoots). In the winter the shoots should be pruned once again (3), leaving two to three buds on each stem.

spectacular sight in full bloom, with its dense masses of rich red double flowers on long, arching branches.

Towards the far end of the lawn a large chestnut tree creates a natural division in the garden. Beyond it is a yellow, white and silver border with tree peonies, yellow foxgloves and imperial fritillaries and, to one side, there are two shady beds containing the Aldingtons' hellebore collection. Among the other carpeting plants that do well in the shadier parts of the garden are pulmonarias, epimediums, violets and cyclamens.

From this part of the garden a couple of steps take you down to the pretty daisy garden, with all its containers and summer colour. An archway through the stable block leads to the formal parterre, whose neat box hedges surround bright splashes of colour in the shape of annuals that are changed as the seasons progress. In spring, the parterre is filled with wallflowers, which contrast with the bright blue flowers of the handsome *Ceanothus* on the wall behind and, in summer, with lobelia. A *Cordyline australis*, with its starfish-like array of spiky leaves, makes a handsome focal point, surrounded in summer by the glistening white daisy-like flowers of *Osteospermum ecklonis*. Unusually, the paths of the parterre have been paved with old stable bricks instead of the normal gravel, and they create a very effective contrast to the brilliant colour of the annuals which have been planted within the parterre beds.

The Mediterranean walled garden, to one side of the house, features a great collection of sun-loving plants, many succulents, and a profusion of roses, honeysuckle and clematis scrambling over the pergola at the far end. Here again, the Aldingtons have a large collection of plants in containers and in many raised beds. As Peter Aldington points out, it is the ideal style of garden for anyone retired, as you barely have to stoop to tend the plants.

The garden walls and trees play host to a wide variety of climbers, chosen for the situation. In the Mediterranean garden they are mainly more tender plants, while in the small courtyard at the far end of the garden, a large wisteria climbs the office walls. Beautiful though the latter is, it is a very vigorous grower and has to be kept in check to prevent it destroying the gutters and tiles.

Because there is such a variety of habitats at Turn End, some natural and some created, from hot sunny gravel and raised beds to shady woodland areas and water, the Aldingtons are able to grow a fascinating range of plants from very different parts of the world. The secret is to do as they have done, and make sure you choose an appropriate site for each plant. Even the smallest garden has a sunny and a shady side, a sheltered wall and perhaps a tree or two. Given the optimum conditions, most plants will reward you by growing strongly and flowering well. You should be careful not to fall into the trap of just buying whatever takes your fancy at the garden centre and assuming that it will thrive regardless of the conditions in which it has to grow. A little time spent analysing the characteristics of the garden, and then checking whether it is suitable for the plants you choose, prevents a great deal of disappointment, as well as saving a considerable amount of money.

CREATING A RAISED BED
—— •• ——

The most important element in a raised bed is the drainage as it prevents plants from becoming waterlogged. When building a raised bed, remember to leave drainage holes at the base of the bed to allow water to seep away. The ideal height for one is about 45cm (18in) as this is convenient for working on. One of the principal advantages of raised beds is that you can vary the soil conditions according to what you want to plant. So if you garden on chalky soil, where only certain plants will thrive, and you hanker after those that require acid soil, a raised bed gives you the scope to grow the plants you want. Large stones, railway sleepers or bricks can all be used to create the structure.

ALPINE GARDEN
21 CHAPEL STREET

● ● ◆ ● ●

W HEN THE CURTISES MOVED INTO their present home twenty-one years
ago, the garden did not exist. It was covered in old pig sheds,
chicken wire and accumulated rubbish. Gradually they managed to
clear the site, and their interest in gardening has simply developed
over the years.

Surrounding the sixteenth-century farmhouse is a small walled
garden, which today houses a remarkable collection of rock and alpine
plants. The Curtises' first attempt at the garden included a lawn, but
this they have now dug up to create a sunken pond, the spoil from the
excavations being used to create a magnificent rock garden.

*BELOW The pond at Chapel Street was attempted twice before the Curtises were
satisfied with its proportions. Now successfully established, it plays host to a range
of water-loving plants, including irises, marsh marigolds and water-lilies.*

THE COBWEB HOUSELEEK

The cobweb houseleek (*Sempervivum arachnoideum*) is an extraordinary looking plant that emanates from the mountains of Europe. It makes a dense mat of foliage, spreading to about 30cm (12in), and produces rose red flowers in midsummer on tall stems, about 15cm (6in) high. You can grow this species, and other houseleeks, in ordinary soil, provided it is well drained and in a sunny position. They look good in troughs and do well in raised beds.

Sempervivums are easily propagated, producing offsets which can be removed and replanted in autumn or early spring.

Cliff Curtis's interest in alpine plants began when he took a City and Guilds course in Amenity Horticulture and building a rock garden was one of the course projects. He likes alpines, he says, because you can have something in flower all the year round, as the plants come from all corners of the globe.

As Cliff points out, one of the key elements in growing alpines successfully is ensuring that you have the right place in which to plant them. They come, naturally, from the mountainous areas of the world, growing often on steep slopes where there is precious little topsoil. As a result, they are used to free-draining habitats. No alpine can abide having its feet wet for too long at a stretch — the crowns simply rot away.

Troughs and raised beds are the ideal growing mediums for alpines because you can control the environment very precisely. Most alpines grow best on light, gritty, peaty soil that provides plenty of nutrients but does not hold the water.

BELOW LEFT Old Belfast sinks or small, shallow, animal drinking troughs make ideal homes for alpines, if filled with an appropriate growing medium. There must be some form of drainage hole in the base, or the trough will become waterlogged and the soil sour. Make sure the trough has a good base layer of pebbles or coarse gravel and then cover with a mixture of John Innes No. 3 compost and peat, in 50:50 ratio, mixed with grit. The aim is to make the soil very free-draining.

Plant the trough up generously — one about 90cm × 45cm (3ft × 18in) would require around 15 plants — teasing the roots out of the plants to be inserted. Firm them in well and water thoroughly afterwards. Fill the spaces in between with gravel. This helps to prevent weeds growing and retains the moisture in the soil — a necessity as the troughs dry out very quickly in hot sun.

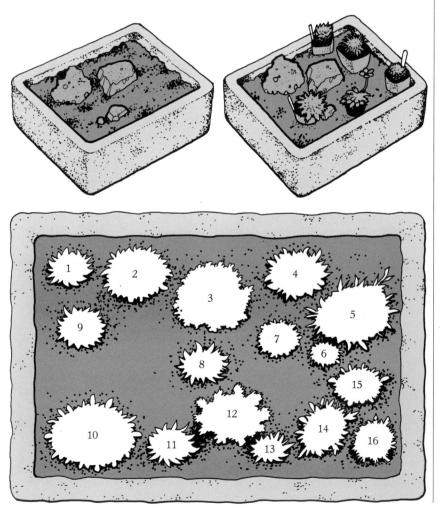

LEFT This is Cliff Curtis's suggested plan for an alpine trough.

1 Sempervivum, 2 Berberis 'Corallina Compacta', 3 Raoulia australis, 4 Sedum hispanicum 'Aureum', 5 Dianthus anatolicus, 6 Armeria juniperifolia, 7 Saxifraga 'Whitehills', 8 Sedum sp 9 Androsace carnea laggeri, 10 Hebe 'Quicksilver', 11 Sempervivum, 12 Erodium guttatum, 13 Sempervivum, 14 Dianthus 'Nyewood's Cream', 15 Hebe 'Green Globe', 16 Thymus × citriodorus 'Aureus'.

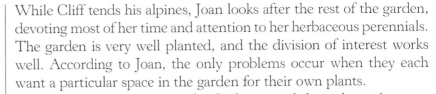

While Cliff tends his alpines, Joan looks after the rest of the garden, devoting most of her time and attention to her herbaceous perennials. The garden is very well planted, and the division of interest works well. According to Joan, the only problems occur when they each want a particular space in the garden for their own plants.

Joan aims to keep the garden looking good throughout the year, and the display starts in spring with the bulbs. She prefers the smaller-flowered daffodils, like *Narcissus* 'Tête à Tête', to the large blowzy King Alfreds, as the smaller ones suit the scale of the garden better and the leaves are less of a problem once the flowers have died down. The Curtises have a wide range of spring bulbs, starting with snowdrops in January and including eranthis, leucojum, scillas, crocuses, anemones and tulips. Joan prefers the Lily-flowered tulips, with their attractively fringed petals.

The Curtises have quite a large vegetable garden, and the next project is to turn this into a potager by making it rather more ornamental. This part of the garden is very sheltered and will be ideal for growing the hot-coloured perennials that are often sun-loving.

Joan Curtis does not have a stringent colour scheme for the garden, but tries to avoid obviously clashing colours if possible. Nature often intervenes, however, and she is happy, on the whole, to let plants self seed within reason. They compost the garden in autumn rather than spring, so that the young self-sown seedlings are not smothered by the top dressing.

In fact, the garden soil is very good. It is naturally neutral and is greatly improved by large quantities of manure from Cliff's pigs and by the compost they make from garden and kitchen waste. The soil is well-drained, making it an ideal medium for many alpines.

Among Joan's favourite plants are hellebores (see page 37). She is building up quite a collection and beginning to hybridize them herself, although, as she admits, it is a long process.

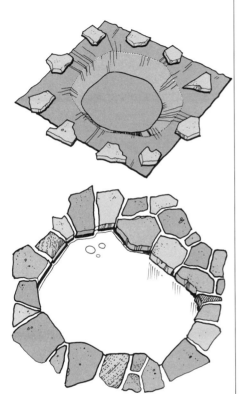

ABOVE AND RIGHT To make a pond, first choose a site that is not overhung with trees. Dig out the pond to the appropriate depth and size, creating a ledge about 15cm (6in) below the pond's surface for plants like irises that do best in shallow water. Then line the pond area with old carpet to prevent any sharp stones piercing the butyl liner. Lay the liner over the carpet and leave a good margin around the pond, weighted with stones. Lay the pond edging over this margin of butyl liner.

COST- AND TIME-CUTTING GARDEN
THE OLD VICARAGE

Gardening, as Susan Hampshire points out, can be an expensive pastime, and innovative ideas for cutting costs are always welcome to gardeners. Meriel Toynbee's garden at The Old Vicarage, Brill, provides a perfect example of how, with a bit of imagination, you can save on both money and time.

The garden is an attractive blend of the ornamental and the practical. Immediately behind the house is a patio, with a large rectangular lawn beyond it, surrounded by herbaceous borders. To reduce the work in the garden, Meriel makes use of a number of ground-covering plants (see page 49) with a background framework of shrubs. This has an added advantage in that any plants that rapidly form large clumps of foliage will help suppress weeds. She allows many of her favourite plants to self-sow, so that the garden combines formal structure with informal planting.

Right Bark chippings make an excellent low-maintenace solution for paths, as can be seen in this corner of the garden, where shelter is provided by conifers and a large variegated holly.

Below left The ornamental pond is surrounded by crazy paving – again helping to cut down on work in the garden – and the raised beds around it have a variety of shrubs – including hypericum, rosemary and Spiraea japonica 'Goldflame' – with clump-forming perennials, such as hardy geraniums.

HARDY GERANIUMS

Hardy geraniums make good ground cover plants, and there are different species of geranium that will cope with sun or partial shade. Many of them have attractive, deeply lobed foliage, some forms of which colour up well in autumn. Among the best varieties are *Geranium endressii* 'Wargrave Pink', shown here, G. 'Russell Prichard' and G. 'Johnson's Blue'.

BRICK AND ROPE EDGINGS

Paths and borders need a neat edge to give structure, particularly in informal gardens which might otherwise seem rather untidy. Broken bricks can be used for the diagonally laid brick edging, as the damaged parts can be inserted into the soil. Lay the bricks at a 45° angle to the soil, and bed them in firmly, aiming to achieve a level, triangular top.

A long piece of old rope can be used to make an edging in a shrubbery, ideally laid on peat bark chippings. It helps to define a border or path edge, neatening the appearance of an otherwise informally planted area of the garden.

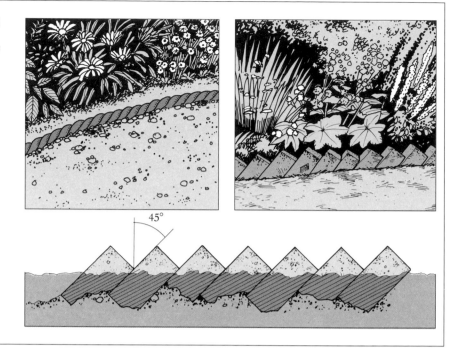

The layout of a good garden will always invite the visitor to explore it, by ensuring that not all the garden can be viewed from any one point. Meriel's garden has several walkways and half-hidden corners, inviting the visitor to explore along the many paths.

For the path edges themselves, she has used a variety of edging devices. A good, cheap solution, she suggests, is to buy a length of rope, let it weather well, and then lay it at the edge of the border like a Victorian twisted tile edging. It works best as the edge to a fairly informal border, between the planting and the gravel of the path. Another edging plan, which makes use of broken bricks, is to set the bricks on their corners to make an attractive triangular edging.

In a large garden, fencing can be expensive. Meriel has been experimenting with a tapestry style hedge, which she is slowly compiling by twisting the clippings from pruned shrubs between upright poles. As the leaves die off and the branches harden, the effect is similar to a lattice-woven fence, at a fraction of the price.

Vegetable gardens, particularly ornamental potagers, can be very labour intensive. Meriel has cut down on some of the work in hers by creating a central square of gravel, which has been laid over old plastic bin-liners cut into large rectangles, to keep it weed-free.

Other cost-saving devices include a small corner pergola for a vine, backed by a high brick wall. A ladder with broken rungs has been used for the longest horizontal support and the bunches of grapes hang down enticingly through it. In another part of the garden an

RIGHT The idea for this fence stems from the traditional laid hedge, where branches of living plants are interwoven to create a dense hedge. Meriel has adapted the idea to make use of her pruned branches. Stout wooden posts are inserted in the ground at intervals of a couple of feet and discarded prunings woven between them. The leaves gradually fall off, to leave a neatly laid fence. She simply adds to hers as the pruned branches come available.

informal rope swag, slung between stout posts, makes an excellent support for climbers. Well suited to an informal garden, it has the added advantage of being less expensive than trellis.

For her fruit cage, Meriel cuts down on weeding by collecting pieces of old carpet, preferably brown, which she lays down between the rows of raspberries canes. The fruit bushes and canes have been positioned near one of the perimeter walls, so that netting is only required over the top of the canes, at each end and down the front.

Although the garden has an ornamental pond set in an area of crazy paving, Meriel has also created a small wildlife pond in an informal area of the garden. One of her aims in the garden is to make it ecologically friendly, and she also wants her grandchildren to appreciate the benefits of nature. They enjoy watching the tadpoles turn into frogs, which they manage to do perfectly successfully in a tiny pond that is simply a plastic washing up bowl sunk into the ground.

GROUND COVER PLANTS

Among some of the best ground-covering perennials and shrubs are bergenias, with their large floppy leaves like elephant's ears. Many are semi-evergreen, and some species have foliage that turns brilliant scarlet in autumn. They grow to about 30cm (12in) tall. If you don't like the rather vulgar bright pink spires of flowers in summer, simply remove them. The evergreen periwinkle, *Vinca*, makes good low-level ground cover, with shiny green leaves and brilliant blue flowers, but is apt to be invasive.

Hypericum makes large mounds about 1.2 m (4ft) high, with glossy green leaves and golden flowers, the size depending on the variety.

Alchemilla mollis also makes good ground cover, with its large soft green leaves, to about 45cm (18in), and heads of yellowish green flowers which self-seed freely.

For shady areas, ivy is an excellent ground cover plant and comes in many different forms. Another plant useful in the shade is *Tiarella cordifolia*, which spreads by underground rhizomes. It grows to about 30cm (12in) and has white flower spikes in the spring. In the winter, its foliage turns a wonderful bronze colour.

HERBACEOUS BORDERS
ARLEY HALL

THE FAMILY HOME OF THE WARBURTONS, Arley Hall was built in the eighteenth century in mock-Gothic style, although in fact the family built their first house there in the fifteenth century. The gardens cover more than twelve acres, and are famous, in particular, for the magnificent double herbaceous border, believed to be the first of its kind in England. The concept of the herbaceous border was taken up in other great gardens, particularly in the Edwardian era, and notably by Gertrude Jekyll, who became famous for the subtle gradations of flower colour in the borders she created. It is the herbaceous border more than any other element in English gardening that has given this country's gardeners their unrivalled reputation around the world.

RIGHT The magnificent nineteenth-century double border at Arley Hall in full bloom in midsummer. Keeping such a large border in good condition is extremely time-consuming.

BELOW This little statue in the ornamental garden is perfectly complemented by the sea of santolina and lavender that surrounds it, backed by the soft pink flowers of the shrub roses. The pink, grey and blue colour scheme blends beautifully with the old rose-coloured bricks of the wall behind.

CROCOSMIA

There are many forms of crocosmia (seen here intermingled with silver-grey *Artemisia*), which are all excellent perennials for the herbaceous border. Their elegant strap-shaped leaves ensure that they remain attractive even when no longer in flower, and there are several species and varieties, with differing heights, colours and flowering times. Height is from 90cm to 1.4m (3 to 5ft), and all forms do best in full sun.

DIVIDING PLANTS

Perennial border plants with a strong, fibrous root stock can be propagated by division when the clumps get too large. You will need to use a couple of forks, back to back, to pull large clumps apart, although smaller clumps can probably be pulled apart with your hands. Trim off any dead leaves, and replant the new divisions in good garden soil.

As the head gardener at Arley Hall reveals, it is no easy task both to plan and maintain a herbaceous border. Not only is it very labour-intensive – improving the soil, planting, staking the plants, dead-heading, and replanting any gaps if necessary – but the planting has to be carefully planned to ensure a continuous display of colour from June through to September, and the heights of the plants have to be gauged so that they range down in size from the back to the front.

If you are planning a herbaceous border yourself, he says, the first and most important element is to ensure that you have an open sunny site, not under the shadow of trees, and that you give the soil plenty of organic matter in the form of well-rotted manure and garden compost. Since the plants are going to be closely spaced, they will need all the nutrients they can get from the soil in order to grow well. It is a good idea to choose plants that have attractive foliage as well as flowers, and which have as long a flowering season as possible, or which even flower twice, producing a second crop of blooms in the late summer. At Arley Hall, a very pretty dwarf phlox makes a good, front of the border plant, while *Campanula lactiflora*, with its tall stems of brilliant blue flowers, is a particularly effective back of the border subject. Crocosmia is another favourite at Arley, with its at-tractive strappy leaves and spires of burnt-orange flowers.

At Arley Hall the borders are backed by clipped yew hedges, buttressed into alcoves, so that the plants have a dark backcloth against which the brilliance of their flower colour stands out. Her-baceous borders benefit from a uniform background, whether a fence, wall or evergreen hedge. Although it would be difficult to recreate anything approaching the borders at Arley Hall in most gardens, the principle can be reduced in scale and copied, by choosing a suitable area of the garden and then planning out on paper the plants you want to incorporate, with flowering times, colours and heights written in.

MOVING PLANTS

If you have a number of large plants to move, it may be impossible to pot them up in the standard manner. Lys de Bray (see pp. 26-9) has evolved an excellent system using cardboard boxes and bin liners. She takes a reasonably solid cardboard box, preferably with hand holds at the sides, and puts it in a large heavy-duty bin liner. She punctures the base with a few holes for drainage and then inserts the plant, in new compost, in the box. In this way plants will survive for at least six months if watered in the same way as container plants.

RIGHT Single-stemmed tall plants, like delphiniums, will need to be staked. Insert a cane close to the base of the plant when it is about 20cm (8in) high and tie the plant loosely to the cane.

Plants that grow with a number of weakish stems can be supported by inserting several canes in a ring around the clump and tying a string round the canes to form a supporting circle for the plants. Alternatively, use proprietary plastic or metal ring stakes.

Arley Hall has more to offer than its herbaceous borders. It also possesses an extraordinary ilex walk comprising fourteen huge holly oaks clipped into drum-shaped cylinders. The father of Lady Ashbrook, the current owner, introduced this to the garden, and was warned off the idea on the basis that these trees would not respond well to clipping. Time has proved his advisers wrong.

The large kitchen garden, which produced vegetables for a field hospital in the last war and was turned into a market garden, became too labour intensive to retain. In its place Lady Ashbrook has created an ornamental garden, with an attractive pool planted with waterlilies, copied from one at the Vatican, and small formal beds with statuary. The red brick walls host an array of climbers, while the beds below house a wide range of shrubs.

ANNUALS FOR INSTANT COLOUR

In a brand new garden, an annual border with a trellis frame behind can be created relatively easily. Try planting alyssum, lobelia, marigolds and ageratum at the front (a mixture of white, blue and gold), with snowy white gypsophila, orange-daisy-flowered *Rudbeckia*, *Eschscholzia* and *Dimorphotheca* behind, and the taller love-in-a-mist (*Nigella damascena*), *Nicotiana sylvestris*, *Lavatera* and cornflowers (*Centaurea*) at the back. Nasturtiums (*Tropaeolum sp*), runner beans and sweet peas (*Lathyrus sp*) could then be grown on the trellis.

A good 'filler' plant is *Cleome hassleriana*, a tall plant for the back of the border, which flowers in summer. It has large rounded heads of flowers, normally white but rose pink in the variety 'Rose Queen'. It grows to about 1.2m (4ft). For foliage, use *Ricinus communis*, the castor oil plant, with its handsome palmate leaves, and for star quality, grow cannas, with their exotic red or orange flowers and purple foliage. For the front of the border, busy Lizzies and pansies and dwarf sweet Williams make a good splash of colour.

CONTAINER GARDEN
TORWOOD

· · ● · ·

S TANLEY AND LAVINIA WOODWARD have been enthusiastic gardeners almost all of their lives. Not only is it in their blood, but they also seem to have passed their passion on to their children and grandchildren.

· They live in what could be described as a perfectly ordinary semi-detached house near Ross on Wye, but their garden genuinely justifies the term 'extraordinary'. It is awash with colour for as much of the year as possible. Lavinia Woodward's particular fancy is for hanging baskets — she makes over fifty of them every year — and they hang from every available place in the garden, in trees, on walls, from pergolas. The restrained, themed container is not for her. She likes

PELARGONIUMS

Commonly called geraniums, pelargoniums are extremely easy to grow; they thrive on neglect. Their greatest virtue is that they have a long flowering season, sometimes over several months. There is a very wide variety available, including trailing geraniums (which can also be induced to climb), those with scented or variegated leaves, and those with single or double flowers. Of the trailing geraniums, *Pelargonium* 'L'Elegante' is considered one of the prettiest, with its narrow-petalled white flowers with purple veining, and its white and green variegated leaves.

LEFT Colour is the key at Torwood and here, in a summer border, it is provided in abundance by rudbeckias, phloxes and penstemons among the taller plants, with busy Lizzies below. Clouds of white gypsophila and white daisies punctuate the hotter pinks and reds.

ABOVE Pelargoniums, fuchsias, petunias, lobelia and nasturtium are the principal ingredients in this glorious display of colour in one of the many hanging baskets at Torwood. The secret is to make sure there is a good balance between upright and trailing plants, and flowers and foliage.

colour and masses of it — vibrant, unrestrained and overwhelming. The garden in full flower makes you gasp.

One of the reasons that everything in their garden grows so well is Stanley's passion for making compost, the quality of which is so good that, as Susan Hampshire says, it is a pleasure to handle it. Almost any vegetable waste can be composted, with the exception of meat and cooked foods as they attract mice or rats. You should also avoid thick layers of grass clippings as they tend to create too much heat, while very woody stems should be shredded first. Indeed, Stanley uses a proprietary shredding machine to break down the garden waste, making sure that no perennial weed seeds find their way in. And he then allows the pile of compost to stand for a year before use, although a heap can be ready in as little as three months. He also uses a proprietary compost bin, but you can make a compost bin yourself quite easily out of old planks or even chicken wire. A good top dressing of manure keeps the compost warm and helps the rotting process to take place as does turning the heap occasionally. People often have two compost heaps: one which they can keep on adding to and one that is ready for use.

As a result of Lavinia's green fingers and Stanley's compost, the small garden is now so overflowing with plants that when Lavinia was given a shrub by a friend recently, she could not find a place for it. Unlike so many people who buy their garden, pot, peat and plant, from the garden centre, the Woodwards grow everything themselves from cuttings or seeds, so that even in the winter they are busy saving and germinating seeds for next year's array of flowers.

In fact, gardening with containers, like hanging baskets, is ideal for Lavinia Woodward, and people like her who suffer from arthritis and find it hard to bend or move about, as much of her work can be done sitting down. Her hanging baskets normally contain a mixture of pelargoniums, busy Lizzies, petunias and trailing plants like helichrysum, lobelias and ivies. You can make hanging baskets using a variety of containers — plastic, terracotta, wicker or wire — and Lavinia prefers to line hers with moss as it looks more natural. She grows her pelargoniums from cuttings, which take very easily, and are ready for a very early summer display. One disadvantage with hanging baskets, however, is that in hot weather they are quite time-consuming as they need watering at least twice a day.

The Woodwards are lucky enough to have a conservatory, where they do a lot of the propagation of their plants and where Stanley also grows orchids. He has about twelve species in all, including cymbidiums, which are among the best orchids for amateur orchid enthusiasts as they are relatively easy to keep and will cope well with the normal heating of a garden room or conservatory. Their spires

BELOW There are many plants well suited for use in hanging baskets, but the most popular are pelargoniums, busy Lizzies, petunias (Impatiens) and lobelia for flower colour, and various ivies and grey-leaved plants, like Helichrysum petiolare, for foliage interest. Try to create a balance between trailing plants and standard forms. The basket, which can be made from wire, wicker, plastic or terracotta, will need some kind of permeable liner, normally foam or perforated plastic, and should be filled with compost. Hanging baskets dry out very quickly and will need watering morning and evening in hot sunshine. To water hanging baskets at high level, attach a stout cane to the nozzle end of the hose. The plants will also need feeding regularly in summer (about once a fortnight) with a general-purpose liquid fertilizer.

of waxy, scented flowers are both exotic and extremely attractive. To grow them successfully you must give them plenty of light and a winter temperature no lower than 7°C (45°F).

In addition to their enthusiasm for gardening, both Lavinia and Stanley are very keen on nature. The ponds in the garden are populated with frogs and newts, and also play host to dragonflies. They encourage their grandchildren to take an active interest in the local wildlife and often go on outings with them to the local woods and bring back compost. To their delight, it has often turned out to be full of interesting wildflower seeds, including orchids and wood anemones, which then appear spontaneously in the garden.

SOWING SEEDS

Most annuals and biennials can be raised easily from seed. Whereas annuals flower the same year that the seed is sown, biennials take two years to flower.

Small fine seed is normally sown in very shallow drills in about 5cm (2in) of special compost. It should be covered lightly with soil and then left in a warm place to germinate. Time taken for germination depends on the seed chosen, but it is normally about two to three weeks. Keep them consistently moist, but be careful not to overdo it and waterlog them.

Once the seeds have germinated and are big enough to handle, thin them out and prick them out into another container, spacing the seeds far enough apart (usually about 5cm [2in] will suffice) to allow a decent root system to develop. When they have grown on sufficiently to look reasonably strong (generally after about three weeks) put them into individual pots and allow to grow on until large enough to transplant into the garden. Biennials, such as the cowslips in this garden, should be planted out in the autumn to flower the following summer.

ROSE GARDEN
ELSING HALL

LEFT Elsing Hall seen across the moat, with the deep pink, Alba rose, 'Queen of Denmark', and large peltiphyllum leaves in the foreground. Roses also festoon the magnificent façade of the hall, while sun-loving plants sprawl across the gravel terrace.

ROSA MUNDI

One of the oldest roses, the remarkable crimson and white striped *Rosa mundi* is purported to be named after the 'fair Rosamund', mistress of King Henry II. A sport of *Rosa gallica officinalis*, it grows to about 90cm tall by 90cm wide (3ft by 3ft). It makes a good hedging rose and will grow in poor soil. Flowering only in midsummer, it tolerates a certain amount of shade and does well grown in a container.

RIGHT Daisy-gone-crazy, alias Erigeron mucronatus, *smothers the steps leading down from the terrace, while* Phlomis fruticosa, *foxgloves and alliums are growing behind.*

THE MEDIEVAL MOATED MANOR HOUSE of Elsing Hall, with its half-timbered gables and ornate sugar-twist chimneys (the latter admittedly a nineteenth-century reproduction, but just as effective as the real thing), makes the perfect backdrop for the collection of more than 300 or so old-fashioned roses that the Cargills have planted since they bought Elsing Hall in 1982. The manor house itself dates back to the fifteenth century, when it was built for a member of the Hastings family, whose father had been Master of the Horse for the Black Prince. The Cargills like to think that he rode out from Elsing Hall to the battles at Agincourt and Crécy in France.

Little more than a wilderness when they arrived, the garden has slowly been restored by the Cargills to its former glory. They have dredged out the moat and the old 'stew' pond, which was the breeding

PLANTING A ROSE

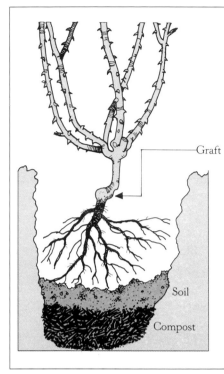

Graft

Soil

Compost

Roses need an ample planting hole and plenty of well-rooted farmyard manure, so dig the hole at least twice as large as the plant you are intending to put in it. (As Shirley Cargill points out, planting a rose is like constructing a building. If you want it to last, you have to make sure the foundations are solid.) Fork a good quantity of manure into the hole, with a covering of soil (the roots do not like to go straight into the muck), and then position the roots of the rose tree so that the graft mark is just below the surface of the soil. Backfill the planting hole and tread it down firmly to ensure the rose is well-anchored in position. Remove any plant labels. According to Shirley Cargill, you get die-back if you leave them on. After planting cut the rose back to the first few buds on the leading shoots, to give the roots a chance to develop.

ground for fish for the monastery. Sun-loving perennials have been planted on and beside the gravel terraces that face south across the moat and large-leaved plants like rodgersias, rheums, gunneras and peltiphyllum have been added round the water's margins.

The gardens at Elsing Hall completely surround the house, and water is everywhere, its calm expanse providing a wonderful foil to the exuberance of the planting. Equally omnipresent are Shirley Cargill's favourite old-fashioned roses. On the small bridge that leads across the moat as you come up the drive, 'Francis E. Lester', with its scented, pink-tinged white flowers, mixes with other climbers such as clematis, honeysuckle and a golden-leaved hop; while a whole host of roses can be found on the house walls, where they are underplanted with pinks, philadelphus, euphorbias, senecio and phlomis. But it is the old vegetable garden, which was derelict when the Cargills took over Elsing Hall, that now houses the greatest collection. They climb up its magnificent brick walls and scramble at will over the ancient fruit trees. Among Shirley's favourite roses are 'Queen of Denmark' (also known as 'Konegin van Danemark'), one of the best Alba roses, with heavily scented rich pink flowers, 'Gipsy Moth', a Bourbon rose with deep crimson flowers, 'Madame Gregoire Staechlin', with its delicate pale pink flowers and large orange hips, 'William Lobb' with its velvety dark mauve flowers, and, the most ancient of all, *Rosa mundi*, with its stunning crimson and white flowers.

It is Shirley who does most of the work on the roses. It takes an entire month, February, to prune back all the flowering shoots to the old wood and to tie in the climbers, but apart from that they are mostly left to their own devices.

As Shirley says, there are no hard and fast rules to pruning climbing roses. The object is to encourage as many lateral or side shoots as possible and, once you have grasped the basic principle, it is, to a large extent, a question of relying on common sense.

In the case of climbing roses, a newly-planted rose should be hard pruned and its leading shoots tied into the wires or trellis. The following year, the new growth can be cut back by about a third. From then on it is simply a matter of repeating the process; the previous year's pruned shoots will produce more lateral shoots and these in turn can be cut back by a third on an annual basis.

Shirley's roses evidently thrive on this treatment and she also attributes much of her success to her planting techniques. Indeed, in her opinion, the key to getting the best from your roses lies in planting them correctly (see opposite).

All the plants at Elsing Hall spread themselves happily in every available space. The steps leading down from the terrace to the moat, for instance, are covered in valerian, feverfew and daisies, some of which have undoubtedly introduced themselves to the garden. Indeed it is this relaxed attitude to the planting, in which nature has been encouraged to play its part, that helps to give Elsing Hall its unique charm.

OLD-FASHIONED ROSES

Roses have been popular for many centuries, but it was not until the fifteenth and sixteenth centuries that people began to try to improve the various strains available. Among the earliest hybrid roses (in other words, those of mixed parentage, not a pure species) are the centifolias, with their complex layers of petals, which were developed in particular by the Dutch more than 400 years ago. Other famous groups of old-fashioned roses are the gallicas and damasks, the albas, and the moss roses.

These early roses were appreciated for their medicinal properties, and were certainly commonly found in medieval apothecaries' gardens, hence the Apothecary's Rose, *Rosa gallica officinalis*, of which *Rosa mundi* is a sport.

ROSE PETAL POTPOURRI

This recipe for rose petal potpourri comes from Trevor Griffith's *The Book of Classic Old-Fashioned Roses* (Michael Joseph 1987). Obviously, the roses you choose for it have to be scented!

'You require dried rose petals from the varieties of your choice, extra dried flowers from plants other than roses, dried and crushed leaves from scented plants, dried lavender flowers, and small quantities of orange and lemon peel, nutmeg, cloves, allspice and a pinch of salt. The rose petals should be plucked when just open, as this is the time when the rose oil is at its strongest. They should be taken off the flowers indoors and laid on clean white paper in a warm room. Mix all the ingredients thoroughly and leave for 24 hours. Then slowly turn the mixture three or four times a day for about a week. The mixture can be stored in a well-sealed jar.'

Some old roses with good scent are 'Belle de Crécy', 'Celestial', 'Charles de Mills', 'Empress Josephine', 'Fantin Latour', 'Gloire de Mousseux', 'Konigin van Danemark', 'Louise Odier', 'Mme Isaac Pereire', 'Maiden's Blush', 'Reine des Violettes', 'Roseraie de l'Hay' and 'Souvenir de la Malmaison'.

ADDRESSES

ALL THE GARDENS described in this book are privately owned, and are open in aid of the National Gardens Scheme each year on specific dates or by appointment.

Visitors are asked to check in the National Gardens Scheme publication *Gardens of England and Wales* (the Yellow Book) for details of opening dates and times.

Location and admission charges for these gardens as well as for all other gardens open for the Scheme (nearly 3,000) are given in the Yellow Book, which is published annually. It is available from booksellers at £2.50, or from the National Gardens Scheme, Hatchlands Park, East Clandon, Guildford, Surrey GU4 7RT at £3.00 incl. postage.

HASELEY COURT, Little Haseley, Oxfordshire

25 ELLESMERE ROAD, Weybridge, Surrey

THE CROFT, North Cave, Humberside

STAR COTTAGE, Cowgrove, Wimborne, Dorset

THE COTTAGE HERBERY, Mill House, Boraston, Hereford & Worcester

TURN END, Townside, Haddenham, Buckinghamshire

21 CHAPEL STREET, Hacconby, Bourne, Lincolnshire

THE OLD VICARAGE, Brill, Aylesbury, Buckinghamshire

ARLEY HALL, Northwich, Cheshire

TORWOOD, Whitchurch, Ross-on-Wye, Hereford & Worcester

ELSING HALL, near Dereham, Norfolk.

THE NATIONAL GARDENS SCHEME

THIS COUNTRY has long been renowned for its gardens and yet, before the advent of 'the Gardens Scheme', few people had the opportunity to see them. The Scheme was started in 1927, at the suggestion of Miss Elsie Wagg, a member of the council of the Queen's Nursing Institute, as part of a national memorial to Queen Alexandra.

In that year, 600 gardens were opened to the public and the response was such that what had begun as an experiment soon became an English institution. The Scheme, now called the National Gardens Scheme Charitable Trust, has gone from strength to strength ever since and in 1991 it raised more than £1,400,000 from nearly 3,000 gardens.

The National Gardens Scheme helps many deserving causes, the chief call on its funds being in support of its original beneficiary, the Queen's Nursing Institute, which was set up for the relief of district and other nurses in need.

Since 1949, a contribution has been made to the Gardens Fund of the National Trust, to help maintain gardens of special historic or horticultural interest. In 1984 it was possible to assist the Cancer Relief Macmillan Fund with funds for training Macmillan Nurses in the continuing care of the terminally ill. In 1986 the Scheme took on the charitable work previously organized by Gardener's Sunday, in aid of the Gardeners' Royal Benevolent Society and the Royal Gardeners Orphan Fund.

Many other national and local charities also benefit from the Scheme, since garden owners may, if they so wish, allocate an agreed proportion of the proceeds from an opening for the National Gardens Scheme to another charity.

OTHER GARDENING TITLES
AVAILABLE FROM COLLINS & BROWN

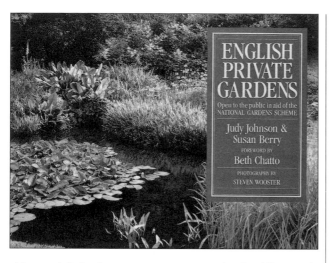

Also published in conjunction with the National Gardens Scheme, *English Private Gardens* gives detailed descriptions of more than thirty-five of the gardens open to the public under the Scheme. The gardens range in size from a tiny London backyard, to several acres of woodland garden in Cornwall, and their styles and planting are as diverse as their size and situation. The book is superbly illustrated, with over 150 specially commissioned colour photographs.

'Beautifully illustrated ... this book is a glorious accompaniment to a worthy scheme.' *Oxford Mail*

Hardback £14.99 ISBN 1 85585 041 9
Paperback £8.99 ISBN 1 85585 112 1

The Complete Guide to Conservatory Plants is the first truly comprehensive reference book for conservatory owners, offering guidance on every aspect of plant choice and cultivation, with carefully researched information and detailed advice.

Ann Bonar makes creative and inspirational suggestions on planning and arranging your conservatory and advises on the best methods of displaying the plants. The book also includes a comprehensive, fully illustrated directory of over 700 plants, with fascinating details of the plants' origins and natural history. Specially commissioned photographs accompany the text throughout.

'To those without conservatories ... Ann Bonar's new book ... provides perfect escapist reading. To those with conservatories ... the book provides the answer to many troubling questions.' *Independent*

Hardback £16.99 ISBN 1 85585 084 2
Paperback £10.99 ISBN 1 85585 120 2